Daniel
"Chappie"
James

Neil Super

Twenty-First Century Books

A Division of Henry Holt and Company   New York

PHOTO CREDITS

Published by
Twenty-First Century Books
A Division of Henry Holt and Company, Inc.
115 West 18th Street
New York, NY 10011

Henry Holt® and colophon are trademarks of
Henry Holt and Company, Inc.
Publishers since 1866.

Text Copyright © 1992 by Neil Super
All rights reserved.
Published in Canada by Fitzhenry & Whiteside Ltd.,
195 Allstate Parkway, Markham, Ontario L3R 4T8

Library of Congress Cataloging in Publication Data

Super, Neil
Daniel "Chappie" James
(An African-American Soldiers Book)
Includes bibliographical references and index.
Summary: Follows the life of America's first black four-star general.
1. James, Daniel, 1920-1978—Juvenile literature.   2. Generals—United States—Biography—Juvenile literature.   3. United States. Air Force—Biography—Juvenile literature.   4. Afro-American generals—Biography—Juvenile literature.   [1. James, Daniel, 1920-1978.   2. Generals.   3. Afro-Americans—Biography.]   I. Title. II. Series: African-American Soldiers.
UG626.2.J36S87 1992 355'.0092—dc20 [B] 91-43503 CIP AC

ISBN 0-8050-2138-8
First Edition—1993

Printed in Mexico
All first editions are printed on acid-free paper ∞.
10 9 8 7 6 5 4 3 2

Contents

As an adult, Chappie
James realized his
boyhood dream—he
became a fighter pilot.

Chapter 1

The Dreamer

The boy ignored his friends as they laughed at him. Little Chappie is too much, they said.

The sound of an approaching plane interrupted the scene. The boys scanned the sunny Florida sky as the double-winged plane soared in from the west and passed directly overhead, casting its shadow on the ground. The plane was heading for the nearby Pensacola Naval Air Station.

Only one of the boys—only Chappie James—dared to speak his dreams out loud. He said it again: "One day, I'm going to be a pilot."

The other boys just laughed. "Oh, Chappie," one of his friends replied, "you're dreaming again."

Little Chappie James *was* a dreamer. From his mother, he had learned to strive for success, and Chappie would need big dreams to succeed. He grew up in a society that denied equal opportunity to African Americans. "I was reminded at every turn," Chappie said, "that I was different."

Chappie's mother also taught him not to quit. It was a lesson that brought Chappie success as a combat fighter pilot and as a leader of other soldiers. It was a lesson that enabled a young dreamer to rise to become the first black four-star general, the highest military rank awarded in peacetime.

Colonel James stands with his F-4 Phantom jet in Southeast Asia during the 1960s.

Chappie James's triumphs go beyond military success or honors. As an African-American soldier, he faced a long tradition of racism. By confronting racism with ability and pride, he helped to break down the barriers that had shut off opportunity to African Americans. By refusing to become bitter or discouraged, he provided an example of faith and determination for countless young people, both black and white.

The young boy who searched the skies was, in his words, "hungry for knowledge, understanding, and a little bit of opportunity." This is the story of Daniel "Chappie" James, a man who made the most of his little bit of opportunity.

Chapter 2

The Power of Excellence

Daniel James, Jr., was born on February 11, 1920, in the coastal city of Pensacola, Florida. He was the youngest of Daniel, Sr., and Lillie Anna James's 17 children. (Ten of his siblings, however, had died by the time of his birth.) Daniel, Jr., grew up in the five-bedroom wooden house he was born in, at 1606 North Alcaniz Street. The neighborhood his family lived in was called the "Sandbed" for its unpaved, sandy streets.

In the 1920s, Pensacola was a bustling port city. Its diverse population included a large African-American community. Since the end of the Civil War, the city's black residents had purchased homes and started businesses. Among the 9,000 African Americans who made Pensacola their home were doctors, ministers, and teachers.

The prosperity of Pensacola's black community was no guarantee of equal opportunity or fairness. Like most southern cities at the time, Pensacola kept its white and black residents apart. After the abolition of slavery in 1865, many communities adopted codes of behavior that were designed to enforce racial segregation.

Known as Jim Crow laws, these regulations forced African Americans to send their children to segregated schools. Blacks were required to stand at the back of city buses and streetcars. They were barred from eating at "whites only" restaurants and from shopping at certain stores.

When Chappie James was a boy, Jim Crow laws required blacks and whites to drink from separate water fountains.

"There were parks in Pensacola with green grass and benches," Daniel James, Jr., remembered years later. "The benches were labeled 'colored' and 'white.' To make sure I didn't sit on the wrong one, they were painted black and white."

Whites often justified Jim Crow laws by claiming that public facilities, though racially separate, were equal. This system, they said, provided the same rights to everyone. (In 1896, the Supreme Court, in a case called *Plessy v. Ferguson*, had ruled that such "separate but equal" facilities were legal.)

Pensacola's African Americans, however, knew better. The unpaved streets of the Sandbed, with no sidewalks or streetlights, were clear evidence that "separate but equal" really meant separate and inferior. In housing, education, and career opportunities, African Americans were often treated like second-class citizens.

Daniel's father, called "Poppa" by his children, was originally from Alabama. Daniel James, Sr., was employed by the city as a lamplighter.

Poppa James believed in the value of hard work and taught his children that an honest day's wage was the way to rise above the unfairness of racial segregation. Not formally educated himself, Daniel James, Sr., placed little emphasis on schooling.

It was young Daniel's mother, Lillie James, who stressed education as a means of getting ahead. Her father was one of Pensacola's few black mailmen, and her mother worked in the home of a wealthy white family. Lillie's parents had made certain that their daughter received a high-school education. They had taught Lillie to seek self-improvement through her schoolwork. This was the way, they believed, to overcome prejudice.

Lillie decided to teach her own children at home rather than send them to the public schools that were set aside for African-American children. When other black parents heard about this, they asked Lillie James to teach their children as well. With the number of her students growing steadily, Lillie persuaded her husband to build a schoolhouse in the back yard.

This was the start of the Lillie A. James Private School, the only private school in Pensacola for African-American children. The cost to attend the school was twenty-five cents a week—if a family could afford it. If not, parents were allowed to pay whatever they could.

"Miss Lillie," as she was known to her students, taught the usual school subjects—reading, writing, and arithmetic—as well as lessons in history, public speaking, religion, and manners. She was a demanding teacher, warmly praising her students' successes but quick with criticism and punishment for those who failed to improve.

Whatever the subject, Lillie James stressed that personal excellence was the key to success in a white-dominated world. Her teachings were really a challenge to her students. "Prove to the world that you can compete on an equal basis," she would tell them. "If they say you are dirty, make sure you are clean. If they say you are afraid, make sure you are brave. If they say you are dishonest, make sure you take nothing that is not yours."

Miss Lillie's school was a popular one in the black neighborhoods of Pensacola. In her back-yard schoolhouse, she taught the value of self-reliance to children who could not afford to depend on the help of the white community. As the years passed, many of Miss Lillie's former students went on to become doctors, lawyers, and teachers.

They were "monuments to my mother's love, faith, and skill," Daniel James, Jr., said.

As one of Miss Lillie's students, Daniel James knew that children learned more than reading and writing in her school. They discovered, according to Daniel, "a sense of purpose and direction." What they learned, he later observed, was "a set of values that sustain them to this day."

Lillie James was the dominating presence in Daniel's early years. As mother and teacher, she took every opportunity to instill in young Daniel her belief in the power of individual excellence. She taught him that "whites only" water fountains and the other signs of segregation did not make him inferior—and she insisted that he should never act that way.

Discrimination was unfair, but for Lillie James that was no excuse for anything less than doing one's best. "My son," she ordered, "don't you dare sacrifice your abilities." If Daniel had a tougher road to success because he was black, then he must work harder than anyone else.

There was no room for discouragement in Miss Lillie's home or school. "For you, my son, there is an Eleventh Commandment," she would often say. "Thou shalt not quit."

Daniel James, Jr., responded to his mother's encouragement by developing a strong desire to succeed in whatever he did. He was an enthusiastic student. His favorite activity, when he was not in class, was playing school—he liked to act the part of the teacher.

Daniel, Jr., eagerly took part in the many plays and recitals that the students put on, displaying his talent for acting and singing—and showing off. Lillie James's purpose in staging such entertainment was to help the children gain confidence and social poise. Daniel James, Jr., would develop these traits in abundance.

Determined to please his mother, Daniel James did his best both at school and in sports. Success, he learned early in life, won praise from others, and Daniel liked the feeling of accomplishment. But success at home and school could not protect Daniel, Jr., from the racism of the world around him. "Everywhere I looked," he said of Pensacola, "this built-in inferiority complex for a young black lad growing up was evident."

Miss Lillie could not change the world where Jim Crow held sway. But by insisting that black children could achieve excellence—by demanding that he do his best—she ensured that Daniel would never suffer from that built-in feeling of inferiority.

As he grew older, Daniel, Jr., began to pay more attention to the men in his family. His father's example of hard work and discipline made a deep impression on him. He admired his older brother Charles, who was a star athlete in college. Charles was known as "Chappie," and young Daniel took the nickname "Little Chappie."

The lives of other black men also attracted the attention of Little Chappie. He followed the career of Benjamin O. Davis, Jr., at that time the only African-American cadet at the U.S. Military Academy at West Point. Watching Benjamin Davis in newsreels at the movie theater, Little Chappie James dreamed of a military career for himself. He wanted to be a flier, like the Army pilots at the naval air station in Pensacola.

In the fall of 1933, at age 13, Little Chappie entered Washington High School. Achievement in school was less important to him than being well known and well liked. Daniel, Jr., participated in school activities where he could use his acting and singing talents, such as glee club and chorus, and he played on the school football team.

"If there were a marble shooting contest, he wanted to be in it," reported Vernon McDaniel, the principal of Washington High.

"He always left you with the impression that he was going to get somewhere," said Daniel's football coach. Daniel James loved to be in the spotlight and didn't mind bragging about himself. "Chappie said, 'I am the greatest' so many times," a high-

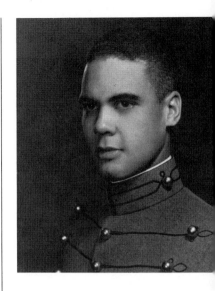

Benjamin O. Davis, Jr., was the first African American to graduate from West Point in the twentieth century.

school classmate remembered, "that he convinced himself and half-convinced others."

In 1937, as Little Chappie prepared to complete high school, Poppa James died suddenly. For days, Daniel James, Jr., was silent.

Daniel had expected to go to college, but his father's death cast doubt as to whether the family could afford to send him. Luckily, Little Chappie had saved enough money from working odd jobs that, with the help of his sister Lil, he was able to continue his education. In September 1937, Daniel James, Jr., left Pensacola for the Tuskegee Normal and Industrial Institute in Tuskegee, Alabama.

"Don't just stand there banging on the door of opportunity," Lillie James told her youngest son more than once. "Be prepared with your bags of knowledge, your patriotism, your honor—and when someone opens that door, you charge in."

At the age of 17, Chappie James packed his bags and headed for college.

Chapter 3

College and the Cadet

At Tuskegee, Daniel James found a school that was ideally suited for the pursuit of excellence. The Tuskegee Institute had been founded in 1881 by Booker T. Washington. Washington's goal was to teach young blacks practical knowledge and useful skills that would enable them to achieve economic gains. As African Americans began to contribute to the country's economy, Washington believed, whites would begin to accept them as equals.

"We shall prosper," Washington told his students, "in proportion as we learn to dignify and glorify common labor and put brains and skill into the common occupations of life." Racial justice and equal opportunity, he taught, would "come to those with prosperity and intelligence regardless of race." The school that Booker T. Washington built in

Booker T. Washington founded the Tuskegee Institute in 1881.

the countryside of southern Alabama was based on the same values—the values of hard work and self-reliance—that were taught in Miss Lillie's back-yard school in Pensacola.

Not all African-American leaders agreed with this philosophy. Some blacks criticized Washington for not directly supporting the fight for social and political equality. For instance, William E. B. Du Bois, the founder of the National Association for the Advancement of Colored People (NAACP), argued that it was a mistake to wait for whites to change their attitudes about race. Du Bois was not willing, as was Booker T. Washington, to postpone the struggle for civil rights.

In 1937, when Little Chappie James entered Tuskegee, he was not especially concerned with these differences among black leaders. He chose physical education as his major subject and enjoyed college social activities. At 6 foot, 4 inches tall and almost 225 pounds, Daniel James was truly a big man on campus. His classmates decided that they should drop the "Little" from his nickname.

Big and strong, Chappie played on the school football team. He greatly admired his coach, Cleve Abbott, a former Army officer. Abbott put his team through a tough training program. Like other adults in Chappie's life, Coach Abbott would not settle for second best. "He taught me how to be a proud man," Chappie said about Abbott.

Cleve Abbott was as patriotic as he was tough. He gave his players a love of country and a sense of duty that echoed the school lessons that had been taught by Miss Lillie. "When the national anthem was being played, we didn't stand around kicking the sod," Chappie James said. "We stood at attention with our helmets over our hearts."

On campus and off, James carried himself like someone special. "We all knew he had something different," a classmate said years later, "and we all wished we had it."

Chappie James was also popular with the young women on campus. One summer night in 1939, he attended a college dance where he met Dorothy Watkins, a senior at nearby Tuskegee High School. "All the girls were crazy about him," she recalled. But Dorothy Watkins was determined not to be so easily impressed. "Nobody could be that wonderful," she said. "I developed an immediate dislike for Chappie James."

When Chappie asked Dorothy to dance, she turned him down. When he informed her that he was "*the* Chappie James, *the* football hero," Dorothy replied, "Oh, you are? Well, I don't think you are so hot." It was quite a setback for "*the* Chappie James." But Chappie continued to court Dorothy, and soon they were dating steadily.

During these years, Germany, under the leadership of Adolf Hitler, was menacing Europe with the threat of war. Alarmed, the U.S. War Department increased the size and strength of the armed forces in case America was drawn into the fight. Despite the military build-up, however, there were still few opportunities for African Americans in the armed forces.

Since the time of the Revolutionary War, U.S. military leaders had denied equal opportunity to black soldiers. Though African Americans fought bravely in each of America's early wars, the armed forces refused to accept black recruits in peacetime. And when African-American soldiers were made part of the peacetime Army after the Civil War, they were assigned to segregated units, where they were often given only routine assignments, such as the maintenance of camp grounds.

The first three decades of the twentieth century saw little progress for African-American soldiers. In 1938, civil rights leaders objected to the lack of opportunity for blacks in the Army Air Corps.

The U.S. War Department avoided further complaints by beginning the Civilian Pilot Training Program (CPTP).

The purpose of the CPTP was to train civilian pilots for combat duty in the event that the United States went to war. By 1941, when America entered World War II, more than 300 African Americans had been trained at black colleges, including the Tuskegee Institute, under this program.

Chappie entered the pilot training program in his senior year at Tuskegee. "I could tell the first time I took him up he was going to be a good pilot," his instructor remarked. "He had more guts than anyone I had ever seen."

However, a few months before he would have graduated, Chappie James was involved in a fight with another student. James was dismissed from school. (He did not graduate from Tuskegee until 1969, when he finally earned his degree.) Chappie took a job training other student pilots. He hoped to be included if and when the Army opened pilot training to African Americans.

In September 1939, the German army invaded Poland, signaling the beginning of World War II. While America would not enter the war for two more years, it seemed certain to the pilots of the

Civilian Pilot Training Program that they would soon be called to military service.

The segregated Army Air Corps, however, had different ideas. Despite the pilot training program, the U.S. Army had no plans to use the African-American trainees. No black units existed in the Air Corps, it was explained. Since the military did not allow African Americans to serve alongside whites, "it would be impossible," in the words of one officer, "to accept people of that race."

Further, the Army made clear its doubts that African Americans were capable of flying military aircraft. An official Army report stated that flight training "required men of technical and mechanical experience." For this reason, the report continued, "the colored man has not been attracted to this field as has the white man."

The Army's refusal to train blacks as combat pilots angered African-American leaders and members of the black press. In 1941, the NAACP sued the U.S. War Department, claiming that the CPTP included the clear promise of military training.

As a result, in that same year the Air Corps created the 99th Pursuit Squadron, the U.S. Army's first unit of black aviators. Based at its own airfield near the campus of the Tuskegee Institute, the 99th was a milestone of equal opportunity for African-American soldiers.

The Army referred to its cadet program as the "Tuskegee Experiment." The program was a trial run, an experiment to see if blacks could fly military aircraft. At stake was the War Department's belief that African Americans lacked the ability to master technical skills.

But, as these black cadets knew, more than their own fate was on the line here. "The eyes of your country and the eyes of your people are on you," they were told. The Tuskegee Experiment would affect the future of all black fighting men.

At Tuskegee, black recruits in the U.S. Army Air Corps studied every aspect of flight and navigation.

The Tuskegee Airmen received practical training in flight preparation and combat techniques.

"We knew a lot rested on the success of the experiment," commented one of the airmen. "So we gave everything our best effort."

The first class of pilots consisted of six cadets, including Benjamin O. Davis, Jr., whose career at West Point a younger Chappie James had followed with such interest. Known as the "Tuskegee Airmen," the pilots began the difficult and dangerous training required to win their wings. Hundreds of hours of classroom instruction were followed by flight training in old bi-planes with open cockpits.

As they progressed, the cadets moved to faster and more maneuverable planes and finally to the P-40 Warhawk, a swift fighter. Skillful and daring pilots, the Tuskegee Airmen completed their training with high marks, proving their ability to fly. And when the Japanese bombed Pearl Harbor on December 7, 1941, it seemed likely that the airmen would soon get their chance to show that they could fight, too.

On March 7, 1942, the first black pilots of the U.S. Army Air Corps received their wings.

Chappie applied for military pilot training in 1941, but his entry into the program was delayed due to the limited number of openings. Chappie continued to work as a civilian flight instructor.

In November 1942, Chappie and Dorothy were married in a simple ceremony on the campus of Tuskegee. "We didn't have a honeymoon," Dorothy remembered. "It was wartime. Nobody was doing those things."

In January 1943, Chappie got the call to begin Air Corps training. He began the difficult life of a military cadet. While the segregated environment and the racism of the surrounding community could be discouraging, Chappie knew that his chance to serve as a combat pilot rested on completing the program. "Suffer a few indignities if you have to," Lillie James had said, "and get what you want."

In March 1943, soon after James began the Air Corps training program, the 99th squadron's first class of pilots, nicknamed the "Lonely Eagles," was ordered to North Africa. That July, Chappie James was commissioned as a second lieutenant in the Army Air Corps. He was assigned to the 477th Bombardment Group, a newly created black unit stationed at Selfridge Field near Detroit, Michigan. There, Chappie would be trained to fly the B-25, a heavy, multi-engined bomber.

In the meantime, the Lonely Eagles—and the Tuskegee Experiment—were getting their first test under fire.

Chapter 4

The Black Air Force

Stationed at Selfridge Field, the 477th Bombard-ment Group consisted of 60 African-American and 12 white pilots. Brigadier General Frank Hunter, the unit's commanding general, set the tone for the group when he called the black pilots together to announce that all facilities on the base were to be segregated.

Separate facilities for black and white officers had to be maintained, the general ordered, because "colored officers aren't ready to be accepted as the equal of white officers."

"He started out saying that they were willing to let us fight beside them, and they were willing to let us fly," Chappie James remembered. "But the world was not willing, society was not willing, and he was not willing to accept us socially."

The African-American members of the 477th soon learned what "separate but equal" meant in the U.S. Army. They were almost never promoted to positions of authority despite the fact that many black soldiers had years of military duty. The James family (which now included a daughter, Danice) was forced to find housing off base although base quarters were available—the white commanders at Selfridge preferred to let them sit empty. And black airmen were not allowed to use the officers' clubs even though, according to the Army's own regulations, social clubs were supposed to be open to all officers on duty at a post.

Many of the pilots refused to accept this state of affairs. Putting up with second-class treatment as a cadet was one thing, but these men were pilots and Army officers. When racial tension and poor morale affected the unit's performance in training, some of the men decided that the time had come to protest discriminatory policies.

They began with the base movie theater. James recalled how the base commanders "had drawn a line down the middle of the theater and said, 'The blacks will sit on one side of this line, and the whites on the other.'" With the cooperation of many whites, the black soldiers decided to go on what they called Operation Checkerboard. After the lights went out, they moved to the white section of the theater. The movie was turned off, and the blacks had to go back to their segregated seats. This happened, as Chappie remembered, "two or three times a night."

The black pilots at Selfridge also protested at the base officers' club. Chappie James recounted the procedure at these "sit-ins":

> "We would start by going into the club at Selfridge and ordering a drink, and the bartender would say, 'I can't serve you here.' We would reply, 'Well then, we'll sit here until you serve us.' They then would close the bar. We would leave, and later one of our white friends would call us and say, 'Hey, they just opened the bar. Come on back.' We would dash back up, and as soon as we walked in again, they said the bar was closed."

In an effort to stop these protests, the Army transferred the unit to other bases. During this time, Chappie was moved from base to base. (Dorothy James stayed with her family in Tuskegee. While Chappie was stationed at Godman Field in Kentucky, Daniel James III was born.)

Thurgood Marshall, who later became the first black Supreme Court justice, advised the black pilots of the 477th of their rights.

The 477th was finally sent to Freeman Field in Indiana. Here, again, black pilots were excluded from the base officers' club. In response, the men organized a non-violent protest to challenge the policy. In groups of two and three, they entered the club and refused to leave when ordered, allowing themselves to be arrested by military police.

The pilots were taking a great risk. Military laws punishing disobedience are harsh, especially during wartime. The airmen of the 477th knew that many people would view their protest as an act of disloyalty during a time of national crisis. It was important, therefore, that the protesters gain as many supporters as possible. In all, more than a hundred black officers of the Army Air Corps, including Chappie James, were arrested for refusing to accept the discriminatory policies of their white commanders. They were restricted to their quarters on base.

As the black pilots of the 477th waited for word about what the Army planned to do with them, they appealed to reporters, politicians, and other influential people for help. One of the protesters was William Coleman, who would become Secretary of Transportation under President Gerald Ford. Coleman wrote to Thurgood Marshall, an attorney with the NAACP (and, later, a Supreme Court justice), for legal advice. Another black airman, Coleman Young, who went on to become mayor of Detroit, typed out messages describing the pilots' unjust treatment by the Army and the reasons for their protest.

Chappie James was allowed to leave the base for mail runs despite the fact that he was under arrest. It was up to him to smuggle these messages to their destinations. "Boy, they'd have killed me if they'd known I was doing that," he said.

Public pressure to release the pilots grew as word of their situation spread. The Army, eager to avoid any negative publicity, decided to drop the charges against the officers.

After an official review of U.S. Army policy, Secretary of War Henry Stimson confirmed that facilities such as officers' clubs and movie theaters were not to be segregated on the basis of race. The black pilots of the 477th Bombardment Group had won their first wartime battle—against the Army's version of Jim Crow.

Overseas, other black pilots—the men of the 99th Pursuit Squadron—were winning important battles in the air. In January 1944, the squadron scored a major victory against enemy fighters at

Secretary of War Henry Stimson ordered a review of Army policy regarding segregation of base facilities.

the Italian seaside town of Anzio. In two days of aerial warfare, the airmen of the 99th shot down 12 enemy planes.

The Tuskegee Airmen had been tested at last. They had proved themselves in combat. No one could any longer deny that these airmen were, in the words of their commander, Benjamin O. Davis, Jr., "legitimate members of Uncle Sam's Air Corps."

To improve the low morale and deal with the racial tension that gripped the 477th under white commanders, Colonel Davis was assigned in June 1945 to command the unit. It was his job to make sure that the pilots of the 477th were ready for air combat in the Pacific.

Davis immediately selected a staff of African-American officers, including Chappie James, to be his assistants. The unit, which became known as "Ben Davis's Air Force," was transferred to Lockbourne Army Air Field near the city of Columbus, Ohio. Under Davis's command, Lockbourne was, according to an Army inspection report, "the best managed base in the Air Corps."

World War II ended abruptly in August 1945, when the United States dropped the atomic bomb on the Japanese cities of Hiroshima and Nagasaki. Chappie had spent two years training to fly the

B-25 bomber in practice missions, but he had not seen any combat. Nevertheless, he had attained his goal of becoming a pilot, and he decided to make the Army his career.

Chappie James had become so good at flying the B-25 that other pilots sought his advice and instruction. Even Colonel Davis turned to James as a co-pilot when he was learning to fly bombers at Lockbourne. As good a bomber pilot as he was, though, Chappie longed to fly the faster, more agile fighters. He liked to think of himself as an airborne

Chappie James trained to be a combat pilot by flying the B-25 bomber in training missions.

In 1948, President Harry S Truman ordered the end of segregation in the U.S. armed forces.

daredevil, a flyer who belonged in the elite company of fighter pilots. So Chappie was overjoyed when, after June 1945, the pilots of the 477th began receiving flight training in the sleek P-47 fighter.

As usual, Chappie James was at the center of social activities at Lockbourne. He played on the football team and enjoyed frequent parties on the base. Chappie's style had always been to get himself noticed. Soon, his storytelling and singing abilities led him to become involved with a base-wide talent show called Operation Happiness.

Chappie was the host, manager, and star of the show. "He was one of the biggest hams you ever saw in your life," a fellow pilot remembered.

The show was so popular that it went on a national tour, entertaining soldiers at other bases. Chappie James became well known to audiences throughout the country. In the South, whenever an attempt was made to arrange a performance for a segregated audience, Chappie refused to let the show go on.

On July 26, 1948, President Harry S Truman ordered the end of segregation in the armed forces. The Air Force, which had been designated as a separate military branch in 1947, quickly acted on the president's order, adopting a policy of integration. "Negro officers and airmen may be assigned to any duty in any Air Force unit or activity," read the new policy, "in accordance with the qualifications of the individual and the needs of the service."

With the war over, many African Americans left the service, tired of the years of segregation, tired of waiting for promotions while white soldiers moved ahead.

"Fellows, that is your affair," Chappie James told his friends when they spoke of getting out. "I'm staying in, and I expect to make general."

Chapter 5

The Doors
of Opportunity

In 1949, Chappie reported for duty with the 18th Fighter Group, stationed at Clark Air Force Base in the Philippines. He was one of a handful of pilots from Lockbourne chosen by Colonel Benjamin Davis to continue with fighter pilot duty. The new assignment gave Chappie a chance to fly jet aircraft. It also meant that he was joining a formerly all-white squadron.

"I never will forget the first night I walked into the officers' club at Clark Air Force Base," Chappie later remarked, "and everything stopped with the music. The band got quiet, there were whispered conversations, and I could see the heads turn in my direction."

It was a difficult moment. As Chappie recalled, "The noise level started to come up again, and the guy who finally turned out to be my best friend bounced off the stage and said, 'Welcome to the club. My name's Spud Taylor. What's yours?' "

"That broke the ice for me," Chappie noted.

With the ice broken, Chappie soon established himself as one of the base leaders. He was among the top pilots in test scores for flying ability. Friendly and outgoing, he was popular with his colleagues. "Chappie never asked for anything special," one of his fellow officers said. "He just wanted to be one of the guys."

No matter how well Chappie fit in, however, he could not escape the effects of racial prejudice. Some of the officers on the base were reluctant to work side by side with a black soldier. But Chappie was not going to allow other people's attitudes to discourage or deter him.

"I came to compete on an equal basis," he said, "and if they were going to try to hinder me with racism, I was going to overcome through the power of excellence that my mother had taught me."

Nor could Chappie's family forget that integration was not always easily accepted. His daughter was called names by some of the other children who had heard their parents use such words. Spud Taylor, when he heard about it, "had a little talk

"I came to compete on an equal basis, and if they were going to try to hinder me with racism, I was going to overcome through the power of excellence that my mother had taught me."

with the mommies and daddies," Chappie said. The name calling stopped, and the friendship between Chappie and Spud grew even stronger.

In the spring of 1950, James was reminded of the danger of his profession when he crashed while flying in a two-seat training jet, the T-33. As flames grew close to the aircraft's fuel supply, Chappie realized that his co-pilot was unconscious. Worse, the canopy that covered the pilots' seats was stuck, preventing their escape.

Acting fast, Chappie threw himself against the canopy with his considerable strength and knocked it off. He then dragged himself and his co-pilot to safety—just before the fuel ignited, blowing the plane to pieces. Chappie was badly burned, and he injured his back. For his heroism, the Air Force awarded James a Distinguished Service Medal.

As Chappie James recovered from his injuries, the peace enjoyed by the United States since the end of World War II was shattered. On June 25, 1950, forces of the North Korean army attacked neighboring South Korea. U.S. troops, including James's unit, were sent to assist the South Koreans in their defense.

As the fighting increased during the summer, Chappie's squadron went into action flying P-51

Mustang airplanes from World War II. The P-51 Mustang was better suited than newer jet aircraft for the mission of supporting ground troops. Swooping down to treetop level, the Mustang could knock out the enemy's weapons and vehicles with a deadly combination of bombs and machine guns.

Chappie arrived in Korea in mid-August. He was immediately assigned to be part of a flight team with Spud Taylor and two other friends from the 18th Fighter Group.

Known as the "ferocious four," the pilots kept up a constant round of combat flying—as many as eight combat missions a day. Chappie wore a black panther symbol on his flight helmet in honor of the Tuskegee Airmen.

When it was his turn to be the flight leader for the "ferocious four," Chappie James was known as "Black Leader" on the radio. The flight was called "Black Flight."

On October 15, 1950, "Black Leader" Chappie James led his flight team in an attack on enemy forces only yards from U.S. ground troops. Chappie called in air strike after air strike on the enemy's guns. He repeatedly directed the "ferocious four" into the battle, in the face of heavy anti-aircraft fire, until their ammunition was gone.

For his heroic efforts that day, Chappie James was awarded the Distinguished Flying Cross. The citation read:

"As a result of this highly successful mission, the enemy suffered heavy casualties and was forced to withdraw from an attack on friendly ground forces. By his high personal courage and devotion to duty, [Daniel] James has brought great credit upon himself and the United States Air Force."

In November, the "ferocious four," including the newly promoted Captain James, were flying a mission behind enemy lines when Spud Taylor's plane was shot down. The other pilots circled the spot where Spud's plane had crashed, giving him cover. Chappie radioed for a helicopter to pick up Spud, who had survived the crash and was lying on the ground near the destroyed plane.

Unfortunately, no helicopters were available, and even though Chappie flew back to the air base to demand that a helicopter be sent to rescue Spud, it was no use.

The next day, American ground troops found Spud's body. He had been shot to death by North Korean soldiers.

Chappie took the death of his friend very hard. He turned to his wife for support and took comfort from her letters. "Unless you've been out there," Chappie commented, "you can't realize how much it means to have a wife like her behind you. Her letters were the one thing that helped me when Spud was killed."

Later, when Dorothy gave birth to Claude, the James's third and last child, Chappie nicknamed the boy "Spud."

After a needed break from combat, Chappie returned to Korea. He resumed flying missions, this time in the F-80 Sabre jet. Before long, having completed a hundred missions, Chappie returned to Clark Air Force Base, where his job was to train other pilots for combat.

Daniel James left the Far East a proven combat fighter pilot. Assigned to Otis Air Force Base on Cape Cod, Massachusetts, James discovered that his combat duty had won him respect from many white pilots. "My career really took off," he said, "because I ran into guys who really didn't care what color I was."

Recognizing his ability to inspire other soldiers, Chappie's commanders gave him assignments with an emphasis on leadership skills. In 1952, Chappie

"My career really took off because I ran into guys who really didn't care what color I was."

was promoted to major. Then, in 1953, he was made commander of his own squadron. James was the first African American to be given command of an integrated combat unit in the United States.

Chappie James responded to the demands of military leadership with a performance that won praise from his commander at Otis Air Force Base. "Chappie is our outstanding pilot, a born leader," the commanding officer observed. "Discipline and efficiency are high in his squadron, maybe because he never expects his boys to do anything he can't do himself—and better!"

One of few African Americans to achieve such success in the armed forces, James could not help but be a military celebrity. As his popularity grew, he was frequently asked to give speeches to young people. He urged them to stay in school and pursue their dreams.

Chappie was hard to ignore when he spoke, in his booming voice, about overcoming obstacles and achieving personal excellence. With a flair for drama, he would often conclude his speeches by singing a verse or two of a favorite gospel song. In 1954, Chappie James was rewarded for his efforts by being named "Young Man of the Year" by the Massachusetts Junior Chamber of Commerce.

In 1953, Chappie James flew to Moody Air Force Base in Georgia, shortly after being named commander of his own squadron.

In 1956, Lillie James died of a heart attack. Despite high blood pressure and other physical ailments, Miss Lillie had continued to operate her school until the time of her death.

As he had for his father, Chappie grieved for the loss of his mother in silence. "Chappie was never one to show lots of emotion," his niece later said. "I don't remember any tears. But I know it affected him."

That same year, Chappie James was promoted to lieutenant colonel. James was assigned to the Command and Staff College, a leadership school for Air Force officers, in Montgomery, Alabama, and then to Air Force headquarters at the Pentagon, in Washington, D.C.

From there, in 1962, Colonel James, now 42 years old, reported to the air base at Bentwaters, England, one of America's most important overseas military posts. "Chappie got on his horse and rode off at full speed in four different directions," joked one of James's colleagues at Bentwaters. "He did everything at full speed."

James was assigned as squadron commander of the 81st Tactical Fighter Wing, a unit that included jet aircraft fitted with nuclear weapons. Chappie was put in charge of pilot training for the fighter squadrons on the air base. Within a year, he was promoted to deputy commander of wing operations.

James's commander at Bentwaters was Colonel Robin Olds, a hero of air combat from World War II. Colonel Olds loved to fly and did so whenever he got the chance, leaving the job of managing the base largely to Colonel James. It was work for which Chappie James was well suited. Chappie's ability to motivate people made him an outstanding ground commander.

"He made you think that dropping the practice bomb that day was the most important thing you did in your whole life," said one pilot. "He would relate it to national security, defense, the threat from the Russians or whatever else gave you pride in performing your mission well."

Another pilot reported that Chappie's morning "pep talks" showed his ability "to make fliers chomp at the bit to fire the nearest rocket or drop the closest bomb."

Chappie James was a friendly but firm leader. He cared about his men and often went out of his way to look after their welfare. "My door is always open," Chappie used to say. Captain Ed Orr, the Air Force physician at Bentwaters, spoke for the other men under Chappie's command when he said that James "went the extra mile to make you feel part of the team."

But James was tough on anyone who didn't do his best. Aware that some whites resented his leadership and that some blacks expected special treatment, Chappie made sure that the soldiers at Bentwaters were treated equally. His message to blacks and whites was the same: "You've got the talent. Do something to help yourself."

In the early 1960s, American military planners were paying more and more attention to the Asian country of Vietnam. A former colony of France, Vietnam had gained its independence after World War II, but the Vietnamese people were unable to decide who should run the country. By the mid-1950s, the country was divided in two: the Republic of Vietnam (South Vietnam) and the Democratic Republic of Vietnam (North Vietnam).

In 1963, in an attempt to stop what he feared was an assault from North Vietnam, President John F. Kennedy sent thousands of military advisers to support South Vietnam. In March 1965, President Lyndon B. Johnson sent U.S. combat troops to the country. President Johnson also issued orders for the Air Force to begin Operation Rolling Thunder, a bombing campaign against North Vietnam.

Chappie James was back in the United States in 1966, when Robin Olds came looking for volunteers to serve with him in Vietnam. Chappie eagerly re-joined his former boss. The two men were stationed at the air base in Ubon, Thailand, with the Eighth Tactical Fighter Wing, known as the "Wolf Pack." The unit flew the new F-4 Phantom jet, the Air Force's most advanced fighter.

Maintenance personnel inspect an F-4 Phantom jet before it takes off for an air strike during the Vietnam War.

F-4 Phantom jets, like those in James's unit, refuel in mid-air.

While Robin Olds directed combat missions, James kept things running smoothly on the ground. The base, carved out of the Thailand jungle, was home to more than 4,000 American servicemen and women. Chappie's job was to keep the soldiers' morale high and the base functioning efficiently. For his work, he was awarded the Legion of Merit.

Chappie's lack of flying time, however, made him wonder whether the other pilots in the unit were questioning his bravery or flying skills. "I know what some of them are saying," he told a friend. "They think that Chappie James hasn't got any guts. How can you be a leader out here and command respect without flying with them?"

Chappie James's concern that he wouldn't be respected led him to fly combat missions whenever he could. One such mission, undertaken in January 1967, was called Operation Bolo.

The North Vietnamese air force, flying Soviet-built MIG-21 jets, posed a threat to American airmen on their bombing runs. Operation Bolo was

Colonel James prepares for take-off on an air strike over North Vietnam.

designed to destroy as many of the enemy's planes as possible.

On January 2, 1967, Chappie joined the other Wolf Pack fliers as they sought out the enemy jets. The mission was a great success. In 10 minutes of furious combat, the American fliers downed seven MIGs without taking any losses.

Chappie James was
honored by President
Lyndon Johnson at the
White House in 1967.

Chappie James was honored by President Lyndon Johnson at the White House in 1967.

On his return to the United States in December 1967, Chappie James was greeted as a hero by President Johnson. At the White House, the two men conferred on the progress of the war.

"It is a good day for the cause of peace and freedom when you are on the job," the president told Colonel James.

Chapter 6

Decades of Change

Chappie James had compiled an impressive record as a combat pilot and base leader. In spite of his success, however, Chappie continued to face racism at home.

After Chappie returned from duty in Korea, for instance, his squadron commander had vowed to "get rid" of the African-American airman and made Chappie's life as difficult as possible. At Otis Air Force Base, the James family had difficulty in finding a home because many whites didn't want to rent to them. Chappie had been called "boy" so many times in the South that he almost never left the base without his uniform on.

Chappie James continued to serve his country without bitterness. But at times his faith in America was sorely tested.

From his various posts, Chappie had followed the progress of the civil rights movement. He was at Otis Air Force Base in 1955, when an Alabama seamstress named Rosa Parks refused to give up her seat at the front of a bus to a white person. Chappie was at Bentwaters in 1962, when James Meredith became the first black student to enter the University of Mississippi.

Throughout the 1950s and 1960s, as Dorothy James said, "people were marching."

Martin Luther King, Jr., (seventh from right) led hundreds of thousands of people in a civil rights march on Washington, D.C., in 1963.

James was back in the United States when, in 1964, Martin Luther King, Jr., was awarded the Nobel Peace Prize. James supported King's non-violent efforts to change the nature of race relations in American society.

Chappie believed in peaceful methods of social change. He was outraged when, in 1965, civil rights protesters were beaten by police officers in Selma, Alabama. Disillusioned with his country, Chappie James considered resigning from the Air Force.

But James had been taught that the best way to improve race relations was to work within the system. For him, this meant promotion to higher ranks in the Air Force, which, he believed, would open the doors of opportunity for other African-American soldiers.

As a senior officer, Chappie thought that his influence would be an effective weapon against discrimination. "If you're at the top," he said, "you don't have to plead the way you do if you're at the bottom."

There were times, such as the days at Selfridge and Freeman airfields, when protest was needed to correct a wrong. "If you allow those in authority their own choice of time," Chappie once remarked, "you find that too often their choice is never." When his daughter, Danice, was arrested during a rally to desegregate a movie theater, Chappie told his tearful child how proud he was of her.

But Chappie was against violent protest of any kind. He was also against protest that he considered anti-American. "Don't you ever turn your back on your country or your flag," his mother had taught him. It was a mistake, Chappie insisted, to be so "busy practicing your right to dissent that you forget your responsibility to contribute."

Chappie James disagreed with those African Americans who wanted to separate themselves from American society. "Don't you go somewhere else looking for your piece of the pie," Miss Lillie had advised her children. "Your piece is right here!"

Chappie was proud of his African heritage. "I think that the black pride thing is the most beautiful thing I have seen in years," he said. But as he commented to a group of black Marines, problems in the United States would be solved by people "who consider themselves Americans."

"My motto is to build a nation up," Chappie would say, "not tear it down." Determined to work within the system, James sometimes found himself accused by other blacks of caring more about his own career than about the welfare of his people. But James could not accept the methods of militant groups, such as the Black Panthers.

"We must speak out firmly against violence," Chappie James said in response to news of racial unrest. He observed that he wore the black panther insignia on his flight helmet. "The only difference," Chappie liked to say, "is that this black panther fights *for* his country."

In 1967, while he was still in Vietnam, Chappie wrote an essay titled "Freedom—My Heritage, My

Responsibility." In it, he discussed his conflict with other blacks about the best way to fight for freedom and equality:

"They say: 'You, James, are a member of a minority—you are a black man.' They say: 'You should be disgusted with this American society—this so-called democracy.' They say: 'You can only progress so far in any field that you choose before somebody puts his foot on your neck for no other reason than you are black.' They say: 'You are a second-class citizen.'

"My heritage of freedom provides my reply. To them I say: I am a citizen of the United States of America. I am not a second-class citizen, and no man here is unless he thinks like one, reasons like one, or performs like one. This is my country, and I believe in her—and I believe in her flag, and I'll defend her, and I'll fight for her and serve her. If she has any ills, I'll stand by her and hold her hand until in God's given time—through her wisdom and her consideration for the welfare of the entire nation—things are made right again."

After he returned from Vietnam in 1967, James often spoke out in support of American foreign policy.

Chappie's views made him a popular speaker upon his return from Vietnam in 1967. Assigned as second in command at Florida's Eglin Air Force Base, Chappie was often asked to give speeches about the war in Vietnam. As always, he spoke with great conviction and enthusiasm. But James was passed over for promotion several times, and he was deeply disappointed.

On April 4, 1968, Chappie wept upon hearing the news that Martin Luther King, Jr., had been killed by an assassin's bullet. Riots broke out in cities across the United States, reflecting the anger and hopelessness felt by many black Americans.

For Chappie James, it was a time—a difficult time—to keep his faith in America.

Chapter 7

The Climb to the Top

In March 1969, Chappie James was assigned to command Wheelus Air Force Base in the North African country of Libya. Wheelus was the largest American base outside the United States. At last, Chappie James was going to get his own command. He eagerly prepared to accept the new challenge.

On September 1, 1969, only days before James assumed command of Wheelus Air Force Base, a young colonel in the Libyan army named Moammar Khadafy led a military overthrow of Libya's King Idris. By the time James arrived at Wheelus on September 22, the base at Wheelus was surrounded by Khadafy's forces. The new Libyan government demanded that the United States withdraw from the base. The stage was set for confrontation.

With Khadafy insisting that the United States abandon the base, Chappie James's leadership and diplomatic skills were put to a severe test. Chappie managed to keep the base calm despite attempts by Khadafy's forces to frighten the Americans. On one occasion, James personally faced Khadafy as the Libyans attempted to enter the base by force.

"He had a fancy gun and holster and kept his hand on it," Chappie said of his showdown with Khadafy. "I had my .45 [pistol] in my belt. I told him to move his hand away. If he had pulled that gun, he never would have cleared his holster." Confronted with an American commander who refused to back down, the Libyans retreated from the base.

However, after a month of such tension, the United States decided to abandon Wheelus. An agreement signed with Libya called for the United States to evacuate the air base by June 30, 1970. The job of dismantling the facility was assigned to Chappie James.

James handled the American withdrawal from Wheelus with such skill that he was promoted to the rank of brigadier general by President Richard Nixon. He was only the fourth African American to hold the rank of general in the U.S. armed forces and only the second in the history of the Air Force.

When Chappie pinned on his general's stars, he received overwhelming support. The heartfelt congratulations came from both blacks and whites. "They couldn't have picked a better man," said Charles McGee, one of several black Air Force colonels who praised James's selection.

James's former commander, Robin Olds, wrote, "The recognition is past due and richly deserved. All I can say is that I am proud—damned proud of you."

James sits in a fighter plane at Wheelus Air Force Base in Tripoli, Libya, shortly before the base was turned over to the Libyan government in 1970.

There were some, however, who insisted that Chappie was promoted because he was black. "I came by these stars by working for them," Chappie said in response. "Nobody gave me anything—I wouldn't accept it." Chappie James acknowledged that his success had been a tough struggle. "I didn't just walk in here," he said. "I fought every step of the way."

In July 1970, General James reported for duty at the Pentagon once more, where his assignment was to keep the American public informed about military matters. America's involvement in Vietnam was the subject of much criticism at the time. Well known for his outspoken support of the war, Chappie was the military's choice to present the government's position.

One of Chappie James's duties was to visit high schools and colleges to convey the president's views about the war to young people. He encountered demonstrators who protested his speeches on many college campuses.

But Chappie James knew where he stood, and he spoke with great passion when he supported the American war effort. "Nobody dislikes war more than warriors," James told a crowd at the University of Pittsburgh. James insisted that he, too, shared

When he returned from Libya, James was promoted to general, and soon he had earned three stars.

65

"Unless the United States is a strong, united nation, there will be no place to be free in."

the students' desire for peace and their demand for "freedom now." But, James observed, "unless the United States is a strong, united nation, there will be no place to be free in."

Chappie often spoke of the conviction that carried him through difficult times. He informed his audience that he, too, knew how hard it could be to get ahead. "I was reminded at every turn that I was different because I was born that way," Chappie said. "There were going to be different rules for me and the other guy all my life. But I had faith and a mother who told me, 'Don't give up hope' and 'Take advantage of every opportunity that comes your way.'"

Chappie's dedication served him well at the Pentagon. By 1974, he was wearing three stars on his uniform. Then, in 1975, Chappie James made history. That year, he was chosen to head the North American Air Defense Command (NORAD).

Located underground in a hollowed-out mountain in Wyoming, NORAD is the central agency for the air defense of both the United States and Canada. As NORAD commander, Chappie would hold the key to the gigantic arsenal of weapons with which America would defend itself against a nuclear attack.

But the position was available only to a full four-star general.

On September 1, 1975, Daniel Chappie James became a four-star general, the highest rank in the peacetime military. Chappie was the first African-American soldier to wear four stars. "This promotion is important to me," he said, "by the effect that it will have on some kid on a hot sidewalk in some ghetto. If my making an advancement can serve as some kind of spark to some young black or other minority, it will be worth all the years, all the blood and sweat it took getting here."

James's fourth star is pinned on him by Air Force Chief of Staff David C. Jones and James's wife, Dorothy.

Chappie stands with two of his children, Daniel James III (left) and Claude "Spud" James.

Now that he wore four stars, Chappie was in even greater demand as a speaker. He found himself with even less time for himself and his family. "We had no time for family vacations," Dorothy James remarked, referring to her husband's busy schedule and frequent absences from home. Chappie always felt guilty about missing time with his family, especially since his own parents had been so influential in his life.

In September 1977, Chappie suffered a mild heart attack. Dorothy, who once said her job was to "get him to slow down," tried in vain to convince her husband to ease up.

Although he continued with his work, James never fully recovered from the attack. His retirement from the Air Force, originally scheduled for May 1978, was moved ahead.

On January 26, 1978, James retired from the U.S. Air Force. Chappie met with President Jimmy Carter that morning. The president expressed the country's thanks to James for his many years of dedicated service.

The retirement ceremony was held at Andrews Air Force Base in Maryland. When it was James's turn to speak, he recalled the day he won his wings. "My mother told me, among many other bits of valuable philosophy," he remarked, "a very simple charge, as she pinned on my wings the day I earned them on a red clay hill in Tuskegee, Alabama. She said, simply, 'Do well, my son.' The president of the United States, my commander in chief, said to me this morning, 'Well done.' I think my mother heard him."

Chappie James finished his retirement speech by expressing the gratitude he felt to the country that gave him an opportunity to succeed: "Thank God for the United States of America. Thank God for the United States Air Force to keep her free. And thank you for giving me this honor. And God bless all of you."

Having spent 35 years in the military, Chappie James found civilian life, in his own words, "a little strange." Adjusting to this new world was more difficult than he had imagined.

James scheduled a series of speeches on such subjects as national defense and race relations. On February 24, 1978, Chappie was in Colorado for a speaking engagement. Late that evening, he suffered a massive heart attack. Chappie James died that night. He was 58 years old.

More than 1,500 friends and admirers attended Chappie James's funeral ceremony in Washington, D.C. Major General Henry J. Meade, Chief of Air Force Chaplains, called Chappie's life "a thrilling account of one person's ability to rise above all adversity and become an example of excellence."

The next day was sunny and cold at Arlington National Cemetery. As 5,000 people watched, a team of black horses drew the military wagon with the flag-draped casket. A riderless horse passed by the spectators. After a brief graveside service, the flag that draped Chappie's casket was presented to Dorothy James.

General Daniel James, Jr., was laid to rest.

An honor guard leads General James's funeral procession in Arlington National Cemetery in 1978.

Chapter 8

A Proud Record

Once, when James was a newly commissioned officer, he was ordered not to leave the base in uniform so that enlisted white men would not have to salute an African American. Thirty-five years later, the president of the United States himself saluted Chappie James.

Chappie James served his country in three wars, but the most difficult battles of his life were fought at home. James fought for equality in his own way. His struggle began as a young boy in Pensacola, a boy who dreamed of flying airplanes. Making the most of every opportunity—charging through the door of opportunity whenever it opened—Chappie James made that dream come true.

Chappie James refused to quit. He refused to grow bitter. He never lost faith in the belief that dreams could come true through individual effort and excellence. Perhaps that is Chappie James's greatest legacy.

Roy Wilkins, executive director of the National Association for the Advancement of Colored People, spoke about Chappie's remarkable legacy:

> *"Daniel James—patriot, soldier, general, the black youth who dreamed of the seemingly impossible—has left an example of achievement for all youth, black and white. For his country he has left a record of patriotism and service of which all Americans can be proud.*
>
> *"Who would have thought it possible that Daniel James, a black youth who entered a segregated pilot training program unit at a time when the Army brass felt that blacks could not learn to fly, would be retired as a four-star general in the Air Force?"*

Chappie would be pleased to see other young men and women carrying on the African-American tradition of military service. He would be delighted to see another African-American general, Colin Powell, serving as chairman of the Joint Chiefs of Staff, the highest position in the U.S. armed forces.

Chappie James would also admit that the struggle for true equality continues, as does the debate

over the way to achieve it. "We still don't have enough black doctors, lawyers, managers, enough black laborers whose human dignity is protected by an honest paycheck," James conceded.

And he would be ready and willing to continue the fight. "If I could write the script for my life all over again," Chappie James once said, "and if I had it all to do over again, I would do it exactly the same way."

Daniel James posed for this portrait when he was a four-star general.

Chronology:

African Americans in the U.S. Armed Forces

1770	On March 5, Crispus Attucks, a former slave, is among the first to die in the "Boston Massacre."
1776-1781	7,000 African-American soldiers and sailors take part in the Revolutionary War.
1776	On January 16, the Continental Congress agrees to enlist free blacks.
1812-1815	Black soldiers and sailors fight against British troops at such critical battles as Lake Erie and New Orleans.
1862-1865	186,000 African-American soldiers serve in black regiments during the Civil War; 38,000 black soldiers lose their lives in more than 400 battles.
1862	On July 17, the U.S. Congress approves the enlistment of black soldiers.
1865	On March 13, the Confederate States of America begins to accept black recruits.
1866-1890	Units of black soldiers, referred to as Buffalo Soldiers, are formed as part of the U.S. Army.
1872	On September 21, John H. Conyers becomes the first African American admitted to the U.S. Naval Academy.
1877	On June 15, Henry O. Flipper becomes the first African American to graduate from West Point.
1914-1918	More than 400,000 African Americans serve in the U.S. armed forces during the First World War.

On May 15, two black soldiers, Henry Johnson and Needham Roberts become the first Americans to receive the French Medal of Honor (*croix de guerre*).	**1918**
In June, Benjamin O. Davis, Jr., graduates from West Point, the first black American to do so in the twentieth century.	**1936**
Benjamin O. Davis, Sr., becomes the first African-American general in the active Regular Army.	**1940**
American forces in World War II include more than a million African-American men and women.	**1941-1945**
On March 25, the Army Air Corps forms its first black unit, the 99th Pursuit Squadron.	**1941**
On August 24, Colonel Benjamin O. Davis, Jr., is made commander of the 99th Pursuit Squadron.	**1942**
On January 27 and 28, the airmen of the 99th Pursuit Squadron score a major victory against enemy fighters at the Italian seaside town of Anzio.	**1944**
On February 2, President Harry S Truman signs Executive Order 9981, ordering an end to segregation in the U.S. armed forces.	**1948**
Black and white forces fight side by side in Korea as separate black fighting units are disbanded.	**1950-1953**
Twenty African-American soldiers are awarded the Congressional Medal of Honor during the Vietnam War.	**1965-1973**
On April 28, Samuel L. Gravely becomes the first black admiral in the history of the U.S. Navy.	**1971**
In August, Daniel "Chappie" James becomes the first African American to achieve the rank of four-star general.	**1975**
On October 3, Colin Powell becomes the first African-American chairman of the Joint Chiefs of Staff.	**1989**
100,000 African-American men and women are sent to the Middle East during the Persian Gulf conflict.	**1990-1991**
On July 25, the Buffalo Soldier Monument is dedicated at Fort Leavenworth, Kansas.	**1992**

Index

Bibliography

Britt, Donna. "Pilots Who Broke the Barrier." *The Washington Post*, August 12, 1989.

Campbell, Crispin Y. "Black Pilots of '40s Charted New Horizons." *The Washington Post*, February 23, 1983.

DuBose, Carolyn. "Chappie James: A New Role for an Old Warrior." *Ebony*, October 1970.

Greene, Robert Ewell. *Black Defenders of America: 1775-1973*. Chicago: Johnson Publishing, 1974.

Gropman, Alan L. "Services' Integration Paved Way for Rights Laws of 1960s." *The Washington Times*, February 22, 1991.

McGovern, James R. *Black Eagle: General Daniel "Chappie" James, Jr*. Tuscaloosa: The University of Alabama Press, 1985.

Phelps, J. Alfred. *Chappie: The Life and Times of Daniel James, Jr*. Novato, Calif.: Presidio Press, 1991.

Poinsett, Alex. "General Daniel (Chappie) James, Jr.: New Boss of the Nation's Air Defense." *Ebony*, December 1975.

Ramsey, Leroy. *Black Americans in Defense of Our Nation*. Washington, D.C.: U.S. Government Printing Office, 1991.

Wakin, Edward. *Black Fighting Men in U.S. History*. New York: Lothrop, Lee & Shepherd, 1971.

92
JAM
Super, Neil
  Daniel "Chappie" James

DATE DUE	BORROWER'S NAME	

92
JAM
  Super, Neil
    Daniel "Chappie" James